ARMED & DANGEROUS

("THE BLACK MAN'S" GUIDE FOR PROTECTION & FREEDOM TO A POWERFUL LIFE.)

CHYANNE (DESTINI) THORNE

WESTBOW
PRESS®
A DIVISION OF THOMAS NELSON
& ZONDERVAN

WestBow Press books may be ordered through booksellers or by contacting:

WestBow Press
A Division of Thomas Nelson & Zondervan
1663 Liberty Drive
Bloomington, IN 47403
www.westbowpress.com
844-714-3454

Unless otherwise noted, all scripture quotations are from The ESV® Bible (The Holy Bible, English Standard Version®), copyright © 2001 by Crossway, a publishing ministry of Good News Publishers. Used by permission. All rights reserved.

Scripture marked (GWT) is from GOD'S WORD, a copyrighted work of God's Word to the Nations. Quotations are used by permission. Copyright 1995 by God's Word to the Nations. All rights reserved.

Scripture marked (KJV) is from the King James Version of the Bible.

ISBN: 978-1-6642-0462-1 (sc)
ISBN: 978-1-6642-0463-8 (e)

Library of Congress Control Number: 2020916996

Print information available on the last page.

WestBow Press rev. date: 09/29/2020

CONTENTS

DEDICATION

Aye "The Black Man" I Love You!

For we wrestle not against flesh and blood but against principalities, against powers, against the rulers of the darkness of this world, against spiritual wickedness in high places.

-Ephesians 6:12 KJV

ONE

WELCOME SON

Say this prayer...

Heavenly Father,

I believe your Son Jesus Christ died on the cross for my sins. I repent. I believe The Holy Spirit rose Him on the third day, with all power in His hand. Holy Spirit come into my life and take control.

In Jesus Name Amen.

Congratulations Black Man! Applaud yourself you just changed your eternity. That quick. You just stepped out of the kingdom of darkness and entered into the Kingdom of Light (Colossians 1:13). You are now officially a son of the true and living God! Being a son of God is the greatest identity that you could ever have. I know the voices in your head tell you that it can't be that easy or I've done too much; but it is! Performance doesn't qualify you to be a son of God; your heart does! God is your Father and there's nothing He won't do for His children, according to His Word, including protect them!

TWO

LOVE LETTER

Dear Black Man,

You are Loved. You are Strong. You are Courageous. You are a **Masterpiece.** No matter what's been thought about, said, and done to you. You are precious in the sight of God. The world and everything in it has been beating you down since the beginning of time; but you need to know that God has put something spectacular in the genetics of every black man. You were created from the dust of the earth and the Father breathed His breath into your nostrils. He marveled at you! So no matter what the world tries to do, you can never be broken! You will never be unloved, unwanted, or unappreciated. You're ingraved in history and nothing or no one can ever pluck you out of the Fathers' hand.

-Be Strong!

THREE

INTRODUCTION

As you know Black Man, you have been hunted since the start. There has always been a target on your back; both naturally and spiritually for centuries. There has been more injustices against you on and off camera than we can count! However, victimization will never be your plight! You will be victorious when you learn how to fight! The right way. Not with the weapons that are tucked in your clothes, but with the word of God that is sharper than any two-edged sword (Hebrews 4:12). Have you noticed that on television, social circles, and sometimes small talk that people want you to stay away from The Bible? You know why? In it is the mind of God, His promises, and strategies that will unlock the handcuffs on your soul and thrust you into a powerful life. As long as the Word of God stays departed from your life there will be no victory! Black Man you must learn to see the bigger picture. When your on your devices and you see the grave monstracities that is being committed against your brother; that look that is in the persecuers face is not human! That is an evil force from the demonic realm invading them (which doesn't excuse the person doing it)! There is only one name that demons fear and its Jesus (James 2:19). In this book you are going to learn how to fight the way God intended, you will renounce curses over your life and win! Normally when you shoot at a target and miss, the wasted bullets fall to the ground; but when you aim and fire from the realm that's eternal the enemy will have no choice but to yield to you. God has never missed and He will fight for you (Psalm 34:)!

FOUR

CRACKS IN THE FOUNDATION

Before you can deal with what's going on the surface, you must conquer what lies beneath. Every explosion that has erupted in your life started off with a spark. I'm sure that you've heard the saying, "What goes on in this house; stays in this house!"(Partically said in minority communities). That is a lie and unbelievably immasculating in so many ways. Some of the things that have been said and done in that house has been tagging along with you your whole life, fufilling the demonic declarations since your youth. Black Man you are not going to live the rest of your life in the disfunction of the past. It's held you down for too long. Renounce them now…

- I reject every word curse that my mother and my father spoke over me.
- I release every stain of any foul act that has altered my mind and kept me stuck as a child in the Name of Jesus.
- I reject every insult that has been spoken over me by my relatives, family friends, neighbors, classmates, and associates by the Blood of Jesus.
- I am who God says I am, I only except what He says about me (John1:12).

- I release every pain that has been plunged into my heart since childhood.
- I reject the numbness that has been operating in my soul since my youth.
- I am somebody.
- I reject the devils' of my forefathers, their demons will not attach to me.
- I renounce every generational curse in the Name of Jesus.
- I rebuke every form of witchcraft manipulation in my bloodline, that was done knowingly and unknowingly.
- I will not live my life through the eyes of pain from my youth.
- Painful words that have been spoken to me in childhood will not ring in my ears.
- I will not waste my life trying to prove the naysayers of my childhood wrong.
- Every demon, devil, imp, witch, and warlock using my childhood against me, be removed permantely in the Name of Jesus.
- I release every tragic memory from my childhood that stays in my mind, God your word says you have given me a spirit, not of fear but of power, love, and a sound mind (2 Timothy 1:7).
- I renounce every nightmare that I had as a child that is affecting me in my adulthood today in the Name of Jesus.
- Every hex and spell that Satan enforced on me as a youth; I return it to sender in the Name of Jesus.
- Jesus I ask you to close every exit wound from childhood, so that it will never be opened again.
- I will not entertain people and things from my youth, that will distract me and keep me in a place of brokeness in the Name of Jesus.

FIVE

WORK OF ART

Black Man you are remarkably and wondrously made (Psalm 139)! It's absolutely no mistake how and why you were created. It was God who chose your complexion, build, height, and features. He created you in His image (Genesis 1:26); and that in itself is power! You were not created to be abused; you are regal and everything about you is extremely meticuous and intricately designed. You must carry yourself as the answer, because so many in the world have made you out to be the problem. There will never be another you; you are not a carbon copy.

- In my mother's womb the Father formed and knew me.
- Who I am and how I look is not a downfall to me.
- I will not face discrimination because of my skincolor.
- I will not receive backlash for my height and build.
- I will not walk around in fear because of my appearance.
- The Lord is on my side, what can man do unto me? (Psalm 118:6).
- When I open my mouth to speak, intelligence oozes from my lips.
- My body is a temple of Holy Ghost, and I will not defile it (1 Corithians 3:16).
- My heart is made of pure gold and operates out of purity.

- I will not fear bad news, because I trust in the Lord (Psalm 112:7).
- I edify the Black Community.
- I am a peacemaker.
- I have black boy joy!
- My voice is an instrument of God.
- My presence commands authority and change.
- Blessings not cursings are attached to my last name.
- I am blessed with trustworthy confidants, who don't just tell me what I want to hear.
- I have the solutions to the problems that effect my family, church, community, and issues globally.
- I will not be overlooked for higher opportunities in the work place.
- I will not allow myself to be tricked out of my position.
- I am connected to the right social circles, and countless doors are opened for me.
- I put God first in everything I do, as a result He rewards me greatly.
- The workmanship of my hands create opportunities for me.
- I am blessed to be a Black Man.

SIX

UNLOCKED

Freedom. A high price has been paid for it, I'm sure you know history of the Black Men that have fought for you and your families, so you could walk these streets freely. Thank God for those matriarks, but before them was {Jesus} who died so your soul could be free! Just because you are not locked up physically, it doesn't mean your free. Some of you have been mentally caged for a very long time. Don't you want to go free? Jesus is the only One who can regulate your mind and give you peace, true peace (John 14:27). I speak to your mind and command it come out of the dark places and be released from the cage of life in Jesus Name. Once your let out Black Man don't go back in!

- Whom the Son sets free is free indeed (John 8:36)!
- I command my mind to release all fear and never return again.
- I will not meditate on destruction and disaster for my life.
- I will not join forces with The Enemy (Satan) and receive his plans for my demise.
- I will never again speak tragedy over myself, even when I'm not proud of my actions.
- Life and death is in the power of the tongue (Proverbs 18:21).

- I will not harp on my past mistakes in Jesus Name.
- There is no more record of my wrongdoing in heaven, God doesn't remember so neither do I (Hebrews 8:12)!
- I am forgiven.
- I do not live in isolation and do not indulge in thoughts of suicide.
- I break every single covenant, I have ever made with the Kingdom of Darkness in the Name of Jesus.
- God release me from every seed of racism that's in my heart.
- Everything that I was taught as a child thats keeping me in bondage, Father reveal it to me and release me from it in Jesus Name.
- Every oath that I have made whether it be with a gang, fraternity, or any other organization that has unleashed the forces of hell over my life, be destroyed in the Name of Jesus.
- I renounce everything that I have watched and listened to that is controlling my life, and tampering with my destiny without my knowledge.
- I regurgitate all food that has been given to me with witchcraft spells on it; in the natural and in the dream realm.
- Every statement of misfortune that I pronounced on myself jokingly, I cancel it in the Name of Jesus.
- I shall not die, but live, and declare the works of the Lord (Psalm 118:17).
- God release me today from everything and everyone that causes me to be caged.
- I break every soul tie of every person I've slept with and wanted to sleep with in Jesus Name.
- I renounce every form of witchcraft that is controlling every barrier in my mind.

- I command my cerebrum to think and carry out the purposes of God for my life.
- I command my hippocampus to release every painful memory that has lodged itself into my innermost parts, and held me captive for so long.
- I will not be afraid to love!
- I will be like Paul and Silas in the midnight hour singing praises and praying to God; and as I do, God will unlock me from every mental cage I've been held captive in (Acts 16:16-40).
- My feet will not travel to places that will keep me trapped.
- My hands will not touch evil.
- I will not watch things that oppress me and send me into blind rages.
- I will not put foreign substances in my body, and wonder why torment visits me.
- I command every chain to break in the Name of Jesus.

SEVEN

MY SEEDS

A seed is an embryo, and one of the things it needs to grow is water. When a seed gets put into the ground it is automatically covered with some sort of fertilizer; promoting growth so it can push through the soil and blossom into what it was created to be. Black Man your nurturing is what your seeds need to grow. The words of a father will always be something that stays in a child's head. I can just imagine the effects it's had on you who have heard nothing from your father; or those of you whose father only spewed poison out of his mouth. Children are a reward from the Lord (Psalm 127:3-5); they need to be treated as such.

- My children are a gift from the Lord.
- My children will see me in a positive light.
- My children will cause me great joy and not sorrow.
- My children will always know that I love them.
- I release myself from every father wound trauma that's holding me back In Jesus Name.
- My seeds will not suffer from the father wound.
- I will not deal with my children harshly.
- I will not degrade and bully my children when I'm upest with them.

- I ask you Lord to keep my temperance cool when discipling my children (Galatians 5:17).
- I will always fight to be in my children's lives!
- No matter how long I been away; it's never too late to be a father.
- My children's hearts will be open and not bitter towards me.
- I will have a harmonious relationship with my childrens' mothers; they will not hold bitterness against me in the Name of Jesus.
- God I ask you to remove every hindrance and roadblock thats trying to void me of being in my childrens' lives.
- I trust you God to protect my kids wherever they go.
- I will be attentive and affirming to my daughters.
- I will show my sons affection and train them to be men of standard.
- I will plant the word of God as a seed to my children; and watch it grow daily (Proverbs 22:6).
- I will leave an inheritance for my children and my children's children (Proverbs 13:22).
- I am mentally fit to be a father.
- I will not repeat the same mistakes that my father did in the Name of Jesus.
- I have all of the finances I need to sustain my children.
- In my old age my children will honor me.

EIGHT

MY CITY

The "Good ol' Days" let's travel down memory lane for a second. The music was playing, people was flooded everywhere, a lot of fun times. It was good in the hood! It wasn't really a care in the world (I'm talking about the good times). Don't you miss it being that way? Your neighbors were family, you could leave the windows opened if you wanted to. You made memories that can't be erased. Only the power of God can revitilize your city again; God wants your city whole! Black Man, God just doesn't want you free, but he wants everything connected to you to be free too. Whether you still reside there or not. The city comes with a lot, the baggage that's buried in every nook and cranny goes back centuries. It's going to take the Almighty God and a willing vessel to undo this damage...

- I renounce every spirit of injustice that has been operating in my city and state since the land was stolen centuries ago.
- I cancel every witchcraft assignment of hidden agendas in my city and state in Jesus Name.
- I release my city from every burden of racism; and command racial tension to evacuate now. You have no place here!

- My city and state functions in the original purposes that God ordained it to be.
- In my city we build each other up (Romans 15:2).
- I wil love my neighbor as much as I love myself (John 15:12).
- Jesus I ask you to destroy the spirit of hopelessness that runs rampant in my city and state.
- God let not the spirit of revenge reside in my city!
- God I ask you stop every plan of evil in its tracks.
- My city will not be poisionous to my health.
- My city is not a toxic waste land.
- Children have multiple safe havens to find refuge in.
- Any individual that tries to come into my city with unclean motives; will fall into his or her own trap.
- My city will be known for justice, every matter will be handled by the precepts of the Lord!
- Evil will not abide in my city and state.
- I will not speak calamity over my city and state.
- I will always speak life over my residence; no matter what's happening.
- I will not contribute to black on black violence in my city and state.
- I declare that my city and state is a safe place to raise a family.
- No stray bullets will consume the lives of innocent people and children.
- I reverse any hex, spell, and incantation that Satan has put over my city by the Blood of Jesus.
- Every witch and warlock that is operating in astral projections and putting curses over my city in the midnight hours; be removed in the Name of Jesus.
- God your Word says that You have given me power over the powers, and nothing shall by any means hurt me (Luke 10:19).

- Every meeting that involves the kkk, secret societies, and gatherings that happen underground be dismantled in the Name of Jesus! All of the evil schemes and plots will be of no effect (Isaiah 8:10).
- I declare that there is peace among the brethren in my city even if we don't see eye to eye (Romans 12:18).
- I will not allow gossip and slander of anything that is going on around town to be in my ears or come out of my mouth.
- I renounce every witchcraft decree that my city will not strive and will always operate in poverty and a place of brokeness (John 10:10).
- I reverse the poverty mindset off of my city in the Name of Jesus.
- Wealth will be generated in my city legally; I will lend a helping hand with no selfish motives or selfish gain.
- As I give, God will take care of me (Luke 6:38)!

NINE

JUSTICE FOR ME

Liberty and justice for all…That includes you too Black Man! What you need to know is that the eyes of the Lord roams all over the earth (Proverbs 15:3). Just because you don't see the downfall of your assailants does not mean that God did not handle the matter! Leave revenge in the hands of God; when you take matters into your owns hands, it only leads to harm! You put yourself on Satan's territory and you and those connected to you become open season for the Kingdom of Darkness. I am speaking from experience it's a vicious cycle filled with misery and regret. It's not what you want. That is not God's plan for your life, He will be judge and jury over every attack against you.

- God is my ultimate judge!
- I leave revenge in the hands of the Lord, and He will bless me because of it (Romans 12:19, 1 Peter 3:9).
- I will not be a victim of systematic racism.
- False charges will never stuck to me in the court of law.
- I will not be racially profiled by any member of the judicial system.
- I will not be a victim of police brutality, and I rebuke the spirit of murder that's opearting in the police department in the Name of Jesus.

- I declare that when a officer sees his co-worker breaking the law he will intervene, no matter the consequences!
- The undercover oaths that officers take be exposed and destroyed in the Name of Jesus.
- I will not fear law enforcement when I walk out of my house.
- The angels of God surround my car in protection from violent attacks.
- I do understand that not all police officers are crooked.
- The evil forces that has transcended from the forefathers of this nation; and that is currently operating in judges on the bench; be removed in the Name of Jesus.
- Every tormenting spirit that is influencing judges to enforce maximum sentences for unworthy crimes, go back the sender in the Name of Jesus.
- Every government official that takes bribes be exposed in the Name of Jesus.
- Every hidden agenda of the government that is planning doom and gloom for me because of my skin color; be destroyed in the Name of Jesus.
- Every member of congress operating in racism be removed in the name of Jesus.
- Every member of the cabinet operatng in discrimation and racism be exposed and removed in the Name of Jesus.
- Every board of education member that is implamenting structure to oppress my children be removed in the Name of Jesus.
- I will not be moved by what it looks like, I only operate in faith (2 Corinthians 5:7)!
- Lord I am asking you to remove every racist government official out of office.
- Every spirit of backbiting, slander, manipulation, and preconceived notions that is influencing guilty verdicts

because of my skin color be destroyed in the Name of Jesus.

- I will receive a fair trial in Jesus Name (only apply if applicable).
- Doctrines of demons that have been occupying the bench for centuries come out in the Name of Jesus.
- Every intidictment that has false testimony and false documents; be overturned in the Name of Jesus.
- I will not be attacked by police dogs or sprayed with fire hoses.
- I will not fall victim to being at the wrong place at the wrong time.
- The law is on my side, no longer will I be presummed guilty until proven innocent.
- Every work of evil that is following a chain of command in the prison system to destroy and degrade black men be dismantled in the Name of Jesus.
- Every secret plan of oppression that is in place with landlords and government officials be revealed and destroyed in the Name of Jesus.
- Every trace of the evil doctrines of willie lynch and the jim crow laws operating in every governmental branch be destroyed in the Name of Jesus.
- The white man is not my enemy; Satan is!

TEN

MY SON YOU ARE FORGIVEN

Forgiveness is the most powerful arsenal on the planet! Releasing people, places, and things that have harmed you adds years to your life. However, we are not talking about them right now its all about you. Black Man have you forgiven you yet? Don't you know that everything you've done God knew you were going to do it; and He still chose to love you anyway! There is nothing you could do to ever change that! Aren't you tired of carrying those burdens that weigh a ton? Your back is broken with guilt and it doesn't have to be. God wants to give you rest (Matthew 11:28)! For every drop of water that has slipped through the cracks of your fingers, the Lord has forgiven you and He has your back.

- I release every burden of "I've could've done more".
- I am not God, and I realize I need Him to fight my battles.
- I rebuke every spirit of condemnation, that has made me a candidate for mental anguish and torment (Romans 8:1).
- God I give your Spirit permission to close up every wounded area of my soul (Psalm 147:3).
- I forgive myself for letting my dreams die.
- I forgive myself for taking my anger out on the ones that love me the most.
- I forgive myself for having a short fuse with my children.

- I forgive myself for acts committed that I'm too ashamed to speak of (1 John 1:9).
- I forgive myself for not heeding the voice of God, when He was trying to save me from destruction.
- I forgive myself for not realizing that I have had always had a Father in the heavenly's, whether my natural one was around or not.
- I forgive myself for making false promises; and at times not being a man of my word.
- I forgive myself for:_____.
- I am set free from the curse of regret in the Name of Jesus!
- I live a free life in Christ, my old nature is passed away and I have been made new (2 Corinthians 5:17).

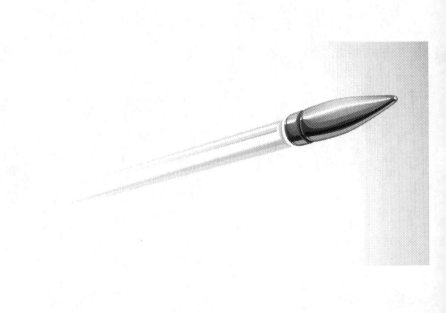

ELEVEN

STRAPPED

Two words: King David. He was ruler over Israel for many years and an unstoppable warrior for God. David, much like yourselves was overlooked by his family and his peers.He was always somewhere in the background, but it was the one that was counted out, that God chose to destroy the giant. A battle had appeared on Israel's doorstep; and the giant named Goliath was of enormous statue and greatly feared. No one in Isreals' camp had enough guts to fight him, but David did! The one that was small in stature had the most heart. He didn't fear what was before him because he knew that the Almighty God would go before him and give him the victory. Needless to say David won; and the giant that was taunting him and his nation on every side fell! (1 Samuel 17). God is the same yesterday, today, and forever (Hebrews 13:8). He is still handing out victories to those who trust Him. You are going to need Him to fight this giant of racism and all the attachments of it. Do not enter another battle blindly; from this day forward depend on God to protect you...fully. As I told you earlier Black Man the Word of God is sharper than any two-edged sword (Hebrews 4:12). This list of scriptures on protection I am about to give you; meditate on them day and night until it becomes your second nature (Joshua 1:8). Always remember the Word of God is your weapon...

Chyanne (Destini) Thorne

- 2 Timothy 4:18 - The Lord will rescue me from every evil deed and bring me safely into his heavenly kingdom. To him be the glory forever and ever. Amen.
- Psalm 91- He who dwells in the shelter of the Most High will abide in the shadow of the Almighty. I will say to the Lord, "My refuge and my fortress, my God, in whom I trust. For he will deliver you from the snare of the fowler and the deadly pestilence. He will cover you with his pinions, and under his wings you will find refuge; his faithfulness is a shield and buckler. You will not fear the terror of the night, nor the arrow that flies by day,nor the pestilence that stalks in darkness, nor the destruction that wastes at noonday. A thousand may fall at your side, ten thousand at your right hand, but it will not come near you. You will only look with youreyes and see the recompense of the wicked.Because you have made the Lord your dwelling place-the MostHigh, who is my refuge no evil shall be allowed to befall you, no plague come near your tent. For he will command his angels concerning you to guard you in all your ways. On their hands they will bear you, lest you strike your foot on a stone. You will tread on the lion and the adder; the young lion and the serpent you will trample underfoot. Because he holds fast to me in love, I will deliver him; I will protect him, because he knows my name. When he calls to me, I will answer him; I will be with him in trouble; i wil rescue him and honor him. With long life I will satisfy him and show him my salvation.
- Isaiah 41:10- Fear not, for I am with you; be not dismayed, for I am your God; I will strengthen you, I will help you, I will uphold you with my righteous right hand.
- 2 Thessalonians 3:3- But the Lord is faithful. He will establish you and guard you against the evil one.
- Proverbs 19:23- The fear of the Lord leads to life, and whoever has it rests satisfied; he will not be visited by harm.

- Isaiah 54:17- No weapon that is fashioned against you shall succeed, and you shall confute every tongue that rises against you in judgment. This is the heritage of the servants of the Lord and their vindication from me, declares the Lord."
- 2 Samuel 22: 3-4 - My God, my rock, in whom I take refuge, my shield, and the horn of my salvation, my stronghold and my refuge, my savior; you save me from violence. I call upon the Lord, who is worthy to be praised, and I am saved from my enemies.
- Romans 12:19- Beloved, never avenge yourselves, but leave it to the wrath of God, for it is written, "Vengeance is mine, I will repay, says the Lord."
- Psalm 138:7-Though I walk in the midst of trouble, you preserve my life; you stretch out your hand against the wrath of my enemies, and your right hand delivers me.
- James 4:7- Submit yourselves therefore to God. Resist the devil, and he will flee from you.
- Proverbs 18:10- The name of the Lord is a strong tower; the righteous man runs into it and is safe.
- 1 John 5:18-19- We know that everyone who has been born of God does not keep on sinning, but he who was born of God protects him, and the evil one does not touch him. We know that we are from God, and the whole world lies in the power of the evil one.
- Psalm 32:7- You are a hiding place for me; you preserve me from trouble; you surround me with shouts of deliverance. Selah
- Psalm 23:4- Even though I walk through the valley of the shadow of death, I will fear no evil, for you are with me; your rod and your staff, they comfort me.
- Deuteronomy 31:6- Be strong and courageous. Do not fear or be in dread of them, for it is the Lord your God who goes with you. He will not leave you or forsake you."

- <u>Psalm 62:2-</u> He only is my rock and my salvation, my fortress; I shall not be greatly shaken.
- <u>Nahum 1:7-</u> The Lord is good, a stronghold in the day of trouble; he knows those who take refuge in him.
- <u>Malachi 3:6-</u> "For I the Lord do not change; therefore you, O children of Jacob, are not consumed.
- <u>Luke 10:19-</u> Behold, I have given you authority to tread on serpents and scorpions, and over all the power of the enemy, and nothing shall hurt you.
- <u>Hebrews 13:6-</u> So we can confidently say, "The Lord is my helper; I will not fear; what can man do to me?"
- <u>Psalm 121:7-8-</u> The Lord will keep you from all evil; he will keep your life. The Lord will keep your going out and your coming in from this time forth and forevermore.
- <u>Genesis 28:15-</u> Behold, I am with you and will keep you wherever you go, and will bring you back to this land. For I will not leave you until I have done what I have promised you."
- <u>Proverbs 30:5-</u> Every word of God proves true; he is a shield to those who take refuge in him.
- <u>Psalm 5:11-</u> But let all who take refuge in you rejoice; let them ever sing for joy, and spread your protection over them, that those who love your name may exult in you.
- <u>Psalm 16:8-</u> I have set the Lord always before me; because he is at my right hand, I shall not be shaken.
- <u>1 Corinthians 10:13-</u> No temptation has overtaken you that is not common to man. God is faithful, and he will not let you be tempted beyond your ability, but with the temptation he will also provide the way of escape, that you may be able to endure it.
- <u>Psalm 41:2-</u> The Lord protects him and keeps him alive; he is called blessed in the land; you do not give him up to the will of his enemies.

- <u>Romans 8:28</u>- And we know that for those who love God all things work together for good, for those who are called according to his purpose.
- <u>Philippians 4:13-</u> I can do all things through him who strengthens me.
- <u>Ephesians 6:11-</u> Put on the whole armor of God, that you may be able to stand against the schemes of the devil.
- <u>John 3:16-</u> "For God so loved the world, that he gave his only Son, that whoever believes in him should not perish but have eternal life.
- <u>Proverbs: 29-25-</u> The fear of man lays a snare, but whoever trusts in the Lord is safe.
- <u>Genesis 50:20-</u> As for you, you meant evil against me, but God meant it for good, to bring it about that many people should be kept alive, as they are today.
- <u>Psalm 34:19-</u> Many are the afflictions of the righteous, but the Lord delivers him out of them all.
- <u>Psalm 118:6-</u> The Lord is on my side; I will not fear. What can man do to me?
- <u>Isaiah 46:4-</u> Even to your old age I am he, and to gray hairs I will carry you. I have made, and I will bear; I will carry and will save.
- <u>Psalm 119:114-</u> You are my hiding place and my shield; I hope in your word.
- <u>Psalm 23:1-4-</u> A Psalm of David. The Lord is my shepherd; I shall not want. He makes me lie down in green pastures. He leads me beside still waters. He restores my soul. He leads me in paths of righteousness for his name's sake. Even though I walk through the valley of the shadow of death, I will fear no evil, for you are with me; your rod and your staff, they comfort me.
- <u>2 Timothy 1:7-</u> For God gave us a spirit not of fear but of power and love and self-control.

Black Man Black man
I'm proud of you
Black Man Black Man
I see what you go through
Black Man Black Man
You fell a time or two
Black Man Black Man
Redemption's here for you
Black Man Black Man
I got so much love for you
Black Man Black Man
The world can't hold you
Black Man Black Man
Dust off that crown it was made for you

What can we say about all of this? If God
is for us, who can be against us?

-Romans 8:31 GWT

Printed in the United States
By Bookmasters